S.O.S. KIT

FOR

DIRECTORS

Supervising, Organizing, and Supporting Staff

by

Early Childhood Directors Association

Illustrations by Ellen Krans

Affiliated with Resources for Child Caring, Inc.
906 North Dale Street
St. Paul, Minnesota 55103

Distributed by Toys 'n Things Press
a division of Resources for Child Caring, Inc.

ISBN: 0-934140-44-8

Printed in the United States of America

ACKNOWLEDGEMENTS

S.O.S. KIT FOR DIRECTORS is a compilation of resources from many people who submitted their ideas and/or services. We would like to express our appreciation to the following people:

Members of the Early Childhood Directors Association who served as a decision making committee regarding all aspects of this publication. It was this group of people who spent long hours in many meetings writing, editing, and brainstorming MORE ideas for various topics.

- Tom Bedard, Downtown Day Care
- JoAnne Copley, First Trinity Creative Day Care
- Virginia Hause, Carol Mathey's Day Care Center
- Lynn Jessen, Paidea Preschool
- Sister Francette Malecha, Sandcastle Child Care
- Cathy Mears, Wilder Day Care Center
- Claudia McPeek, Rainbow School
- Jennie Peifer, A Children's Place
- Rhoda Redleaf, St. Paul Schools and RCC
- Linda Ruesch (Committee Chair), North Como Nursery School
- Mary Szlaius, Woodview Terrace Montessori
- Janice Weum, College of St. Catherine Early Childhood Center

Coordination, facilitation, writing and production management:

- Sue Baldwin, Staff Coordinator for the Early Childhood Directors Association - Facilitating, Writing, and Production Management
- Jill Hix - Editing
- Rhoda Redleaf - Writing
- Linda Ruesch, Virginia Hause, and Mary Szlaius - Proofreading
- Ellen Krans - Illustrations
- Janice Weum - Data Compilation
- Cecilia Meade - Computerization

CONTRIBUTORS

The following members of the Early Childhood Directors Association who attended brainstorming sessions to suggest possible solutions for the various topics.:

- Ardis Kysar
- Linda Ruesch
- Janice Weum
- Sister Francette Malecha
- Daphyn Nordeen
- Mary Beth Leifeld
- Claudia McPeek
- Rhoda Redleaf
- Tom Bedard
- Lynn Jessen
- Virginia Hause
- Cathy Mears
- JoAnne Copley
- Jennie Peifer
- Mary Willard
- Alice Marks
- Jo Kircher
- Jackie Spies
- Phyllis Ettinger
- Barbara Wigstadt
- Mira Jejurikar
- Carol Brennan
- Barbara O'Sullivan
- Lori Haaland
- Jackie Nord
- Mary Oswald
- Casey Johnson
- Mary Szlaius
- Betty Felipe
- Pat Landy
- Ida Mae Sonek
- Shirley Moore
- Tina Liiste
- Susan Finkel
- Jean Anderson
- Lynn Shafer
- Sally Triske
- Charlyn Tesdahl
- Sara Thompson
- Barbara Nelson
- Cindy Kollander
- Esther Patterson
- Leanne Sponsel
- Neil Johnson
- Sue Baldwin

TABLE OF CONTENTS

INTRODUCTION

The Early Childhood Directors Association is a professional organization designed for early childhood directors and administrators. Current membership includes one hundred and five nursery school and child care center directors, primarily from the state of Minnesota, but also some out-state members. The sharing of creative ideas and experiences has been a function of the group since its inception, fourteen years ago.

Through mutual support and the constantly improving skills of our members, the Early Childhood Directors Association makes a positive contribution to the quality of child care in our community.

The ideas and suggestions contained in this book are the results of many brainstorming sessions held throughout the metropolitan St. Paul/Minneapolis area. The directors who participated in these sessions are found under the list of contributors.

We certainly hope that the solutions in **S.O.S. KIT FOR DIRECTORS** prove useful to you and help make your job a bit easier and better!

ABOUT S.O.S. KIT FOR DIRECTORS

A funny thing happened to our Directors' Association during our annual program evaluation. We discovered that our most popular meetings were those which invited directors to come and talk over problems and brainstorm solutions. Invariably, members described these meetings as the ones most personally helpful and the reason they are attracted to our association.

It was a short step from that discovery to the realization by our publication committee that directors everywhere would probably love to eavesdrop on these meetings. That is exactly what this book does. It compiles questions directors have raised and the varied responses offered by other assembled directors. It describes things they have felt, done or thought about in similar situations. As in all brainstorming, not all the ideas are relevant in every situation. And some were offered as comic relief to the very real pressure all directors experience.

Not too surprisingly, the largest number of questions raised at these meetings focused on staff-related issues. With this in mind, the title S.O.S. (Supervising, Organizing and Supporting) was derived from a catagorization of those questions into three areas with which every director must be concerned. Unlike most books on supervision and management, with lengthy chapters of general principles, underlying philosophies and implications, this book just lists possible action steps in "director's shorthand". Most questions offer at least 10 different suggestions listed in relatively random order with no discussion about their relative merit. It is not the purpose of this book to offer step-by-step instructions to be followed literally. Rather, it is intended to provide a wide range of options to consider and to allow you to see what has worked for others and might work for you as well.

Many of the suggestions offered came from the required written personnel policies of various early childhood programs in Minnesota. Some of these are further referenced in the Appendix. We would urge other directors to consider changing or updating written forms you may have with any relevant information from this book.

COMMANDMENTS FOR EARLY CHILDHOOD DIRECTORS

(Directors need more than ten!)

1. Model
2. Be open
3. Set personal limits
4. Observe
5. Listen
6. Decide
7. Act/react
8. Evaluate
9. Have clear expectations
10. Reward
11. Motivate
12. Seek support
13. Delegate
14. Document (...then shred)
15. CYA (Cover Your Anatomy)

SUPERVISING

SUPERVISION

This section deals with the professional relationship the director establishes with each member of the staff. The initial phase of supervision is concerned with making job responsibilities clear and setting the ground rules for operating as a staff member. Ongoing supervision focuses on ways of ensuring program quality and facilitating staff growth as an effective team. Continual assessment and evaluation are important steps in that process. The final phase of supervision is concerned with ensuring smooth transitions as people leave programs.

All directors in our brainstorming sessions held regularly scheduled individual conferences with all staff members they supervise. Although more frequent during the initial phase, conferences continued on a regular basis throughout the year. This is so much standard operating procedure that it was assumed to be a practice all directors use or would adopt. What these questions cover are issues and concerns which would be presented during these supervisory conferences. Note that these conferences are in addition to regularly scheduled evaluations. However, most directors use the conference process to work toward building positive evaluations.

In addition to formal conferencing, directors do a lot of supervising by walking around, observing, and being available when necessary. They are usually aware of things happening with their staff and feel it is important to investigate concerns promptly and respond in a thoughtful and timely manner.

Supervision is a dynamic process, continually challenging and hopefully more rewarding than demanding. It is crucial to the primary goal: development of a quality program.

I. ORIENTATION/PROBATION

1.* What do you include in your orientations?

- give them a tour of the center; (refer to sample checklist in Appendix)
- tell them the history and philosophy of the center
- give them a staff handbook, including emergency procedures, personnel policies
- give them necessary forms to complete--in-service form, staff information form, medical/health form, etc.
- arrange for them to have time in the classroom with the person they are replacing or immediate supervisor
- provide organizational chart
- review job description
- give them center brochure and parent handbook
- review financial procedures
- explain evaluation procedures

*See Appendix

2. How do you structure the initial employment period and what do you look for?

- consider employee temporary for designated time period (2-4 months)
- structure frequent observations & conferences during first few months
- get around to classroom weekly
- do casual walk-in observations
- observe during different parts of the day
- have classroom doors open to aid in casual observations
- do observation from hallway
- from director's office, listen to voice level of new staff person, interactions between staff person and children, and interactions between new person and other staff
- note how they act with children and whether they seem to be on the childrens' level
- check with other staff and ask for their observations of the new staff person
- ask staff specific questions about the new staff person's performance
- try to be "a mouse in the corner" in the teacher's lounge
- bring in a "trained" outside person (from board, council, etc.) to formally observe the new staff person.
- weight heavily complaints from parents and staff during probationary period

3. How do you involve other staff in the initial employment period?

- co-planning between existing and new staff
- get input on evaluation
- peer evaluation
- have person do self-evaluation and compare
- ask well established staff member to take the new person "under their wing"
- have staff provide informal training in areas of special interest or expertise
- have staff include new members in conferences or workshops.

II. EVALUATIONS

4. What staff evaluation process do you use?

- subordinate staff and teachers evaluate each other
- give staff evaluation form for peers; ask that responses be typed
- ask for input on the evaluation process and how individuals feel they are treated in the program
- supervisor evaluates
- checklist at advisory conference given to parents to evaluate
- self evaluation

5. How do you determine which teachers receive merit increases or bonuses?

- observe and document above average work
- assess above and beyond duty performances
- determine availability by state of the budget
- reward assuming leadership role
- reward behind the scenes work
- reward attitude and effort
- reward motivation for growth and improvement
- reward longevity
- reward willingness to help others

6. How do you prepare and conduct touchy evaluations?

- prepare self--psych yourself up, 30 minutes private time
- prepare person--long before, let person know problems and expectations
- be clear with communication, use specifics and examples
- ask for feedback
- sum up at end; make sure expectations are understood
- set up a contract--these things must be done...
- document! as soon as problem is recognized, document attempts to correct; give to person before you meet with them
- have them take notes, and you approve at end--ensures clear understanding as well as provides documentation
- check with person throughout--how are you feeling about this? Be sure they haven't tuned out
- ask open ended questions. What can you do in the future? How can others help you out?
- provide comfortable, private, uninterrupted setting
- timing is important---meet at end of shift or end of day; or pick a day when staffing is adequate in case person leaves abruptly
- Friday could be a good day--gives person space and time to reflect

7. Evaluations can hurt--what can you do?

- reflective listening; good listening skills
- start and end with strong points
- make critical statements in positive terms
- empathize
- offer areas of possible support; suggest ways to make it better
- be specific
- explain how weakness relates to goals and objectives of center; differentiate between character limitations and program needs
- clarify process:
    1) talk
    2) develop staff development plan,focusing on behavior
    3) put on suspension
    4) terminate
- if appropriate, offer support in physical way (i.e.: pat on the hand or shoulder)

8. How and by whom is the director evaluated?

- teacher/directors may be evaluated by peers
- teachers and auxiliary staff
- evaluate self and have staff evaluate; compare answers
- personnel committee
- parents
- board of directors
- have staff and/or parents complete standard evaluation form
- preferably, only those with high opinions

9. **What items are important in evaluating the director?**

- flexibility
- availability
- respect for staff
- communication skills
- style of management--fair, non-biased treatment of staff
- management style in crisis
- awareness of own limitations
- awareness of body language
- awareness of voice under certain circumstances
- knowledge of own management style and consistency
- sense of humor, ability to have fun
- patience
- knowledge of stress level and effectiveness under stress
- knowledge of the job
- ability to facilitate growth in staff

III. STAFFING CONFLICT/GRIEVANCE

10. How do you deal with staff conflict?

- mediate; help both
- talk to each separately, then together
- facilitate negotiation process
- listen to both sides
- reorganize staff structure as a way of prevention before conflict occurs
- prevent conflict by attempting to deal with all staff on equal basis
- share ideas
- bring in an outside consultant
- at staff meeting, allow time to discuss current problems
- when new person starts, go over daily schedule frequently, step-by-step
- do an in-service training on team-building, with an outside resource person
- have a staff meeting with an open agenda
- take two staff people out to lunch (non-threatening environment)
- if petty, let them handle it themselves
- director determines "bottom lines"--sets limits

11. What are some clues that problems might be arising?

- excessive complaints from a particular segment of the staff
- excessive sick days
- staff stops talking when director walks in
- staff not talking to each other
- noise level increases in the classroom
- parents bunch in the hallway/parking lot whispering
- anonymous notes left on director's desk or on answering machine
- silence at staff meeting when a particular issue is brought up
- staff bunching in hallways; whispering
- general negative attitude by staff

12. What are the most common grievances and what do you do about them?

- children coming early
  - keep door locked until opening time
  - charge "early fee" (similar to late fee)

- children coming late for breakfast/beginning of session
  - communicate consequences to parent

- parents picking up late at end of day
  - one warning, then next time charge $5.00 late fee, after three times, ask to leave center (then talk to director/social services to get back in)
  - staff doesn't confront parents regarding late fee, instead secretary or bookkeeper bills parents
  - staff person collects late fee and keeps to compensate for staying late
  - staff person comes in later the next day to compensate for staying late

- staff cannot answer phone while with children
  - get answering machine
  - have auxiliary staff answer phone

- staff never knows where director is
  - get beeper
  - inform staff of schedule
  - maintain desk calendar

- staff complains about sharing equipment between rooms and in building
  - give morale speeches
  - encourage borrowing back and forth so all can benefit from variety of materials
  - buy locking storage cabinets
  - allow individual classroom spending accounts

- staff doesn't like to move from room to room
  - evaluate program schedule with staff
  - hire floaters to be available so regular staff members don't have to shift

- director expects excessive participation by staff in meetings
  - explain expectations at beginning of year
  - ask staff to attend meetings on a rotating basis so all don't have to attend every time
  - use more written communication (memos, daily journals, logbook)
  - plan more effective and concise meetings

- expectations are greater for part-time staff versus full-time staff (all expected to attend all the meetings)
  - add time to part-time staff contract (i. e.: pay half-time person more than half of full-time person)
  - give extra comp time to part-time person
  - expect half-time staff to attend half of meetings under contract, offer compensation or comp time for extra participation

13.* What approach do you take when issuing warnings to staff?

- observe and document using specific illustrations
- call them in and have a private meeting, in a non-threatening way
- meet with them, put it in writing, and both sign it
- give warning immediately--don't wait until it becomes a crisis situation
- quote written staff policy when appropriate
- after warning is issued, set up a two week goal and a follow-through meeting
- issue an actual "pink slip" of paper ("warning") and enclose it in an envelope
- give the individual a chance to respond privately
- talk to personnel director in another business for ideas on ways to approach staff
- ask for feed-back from directors' support group

*See Appendix

14. How do you turn a grievance procedure into a positive event?

- become flexible and creative; use creative problem-solving
- do everything possible for employee to prove self; bring up the positives about the person
- involve self with the staff person (i. e.: "We can work on this together" "Thank you for discussing this with me.")
- keep the process from becoming personal
- investigate: Interview staff separately and determine if the grievance is valid
- try to work out grievance on the level it occurs (teacher to teacher, then teacher to director if that doesn't work out)
- document all grievance procedures, meetings, end results, etc.
- director recognizes the time when "the buck stops here", steps in and ends situation
- a grievance about policy or procedure should be put on agenda for staff meeting
- a staff to staff grievance--interview separately, then bring those involved together to try to work it out
- a complaint from a parent about a staff person--director talks first to parent, then staff person, then director asks parent and staff person to meet together; document!
- a grievance against director from staff or parent--director removes self as mediator and brings in a third party (board member, member of education council, etc.)

15. What do you do about complaints and gossip from other staff?

- nip it in the bud
- make a decision to either react or ignore
- listen to them, assure them it will be looked into, and then follow through
- ask for specific documentation/facts
- talk with more than complainer--consult with others, without mentioning names (i.e.: "Have you observed....")
- do careful observation and documentation yourself
- have direct confrontations, meet with both parties
- add issue to staff meeting agenda
- get in-service training on issue
- if complainer is upset, try to diffuse anger
- ask complainer how they are dealing with the situation
- weigh the validity of the complaint; keep it in perspective

16. What do you do about complaints about staff from parents?

- meet it head on
- act quickly, do not ignore
- gather the facts from the parents in a private meeting
- have teacher respond to parent--a written note or a phone call
- remain open and non-judgmental; investigate and get the facts
- get support from outside sources, peer professionals
- recognize parent need for reassurance
- remember follow-up is important

IV. SPECIFIC STAFF PROBLEMS

17. What do you do with chronic complainers and egotistical staff members?

- send them to visit a really horrible center
- document
- turn complaint around and ask for three alternative suggestions
- be a good listener to those who need just to talk and be heard
- have a statue of a "listening ear" on director's desk
- create a channel for constructive complaining (time at staff meeting, add to agenda)
- confront--"I hear...."
- define who owns the problem
- set up problem solving workshop for staff
- send to class on assertiveness training so they can confront others more easily and leave you alone
- use preventive measure: go to person before problem gets too big
- provide opportunity to give positive comments in a creative way; for example, an apple tree with a positive comment on each staff
- respond to complaint fast--"What do you need to feel better?"

18. What do you do with an unhappy staff person?

- ask what, if any, work change would be of assistance
- if it affects work, tell them to handle it--encourage leave of absence or other options
- if personal, encourage counseling or other professional help
- rearrange schedule/duties so person can be away from usual responsibilities
- encourage mental health/personal leave days
- try to modify environment (i.e.: lower staff ratio)
- if burn-out, try "perks"; have them look at another center
- provide a block of personal time for staff support
- recognize--confront, be sensitive
- organize additional staff support
- pull in outside help--community referral service
- set policy on how to deal with personal crises
- respect privacy
- change, cut hours
- request parent support (professional, personal)
- set aside a block of time each day for staff to come into office
- give real help (i.e.: if purse was stolen, chip in and buy a new one)
- if chronically unhappy, suggest a career change

19. How do you deal with marginal staff (those who do only what needs to be done and/or as little as possible)?

- use a 1-10 rating scale to measure:
  1. attitude
  2. interaction with peers
  3. interaction with children
  4. lesson planning and implementation
  5. classroom maintenance

  reward with bonus if high on scale
- change job duty
- counsel, then out
- specialized training
- specific duties redefined/clarified
- document activity or lack of it
- video tape and critique
- ask them to write what their job is--compare with director's description
- ask them to write what they like/dislike about their job
- use a professional development plan
- zero in on needs/needs assessment
- pinpoint area of need
- if personal issues, refer for counseling
- set up clear evaluation process; if necessary, counsel them out

20. How do you handle problem characteristics within individual staff (i.e.: gossiping, negativism, bad attitude)?

- identify problem and document
- nip it in the bud; do not ignore
- help them recognize specific problem; bring it to their attention
- include in their evaluation and do follow-up
- encourage other staff members to confront or call their attention to the negative attitude
- recommend counseling if needed
- try to identify the source of the problem
- try different staff pairing
- recommend different job
- plan staff in-service on the problem issues, using outside consultant if possible
- help individual set personal written goals
- reward positive attitudes among staff

21. How do you deal with staff who make life miserable for the director?

- let staff know you are not accountable to them
- practice active listening
- don't become defensive
- respond in a matter-of-fact way, without anger or sarcasm
- seek support from peer directors
- draw the lines of authority
- give staff an organizational flow chart
- encourage them to file a grievance if there is a serious problem
- define limits and boundaries between administrative and program staff
- encourage staff to define the problem and offer a solution (no gripes allowed)
- involve an outside mediator
- acknowledge that if there's so much resentment, this particular job/center is not fulfilling their needs; counsel person out of the job

22. How do you deal with a teacher who dresses inappropriately?

- set a dress code
- state expectations at the interview
- provide smocks and nametags
- keep an extra change of clothes on hand
- send them home and have them pay for their own substitute while they are absent
- provide polo shirts with the center logo on them
- provide center uniform at low cost
- use video-taping so they can see how they look
- director should model appropriate clothing

23. What do you do when there are cliques among staff members?

- evaluate how it affects the program
- decide whether to act or ignore
- provide an in-service on team-building
- reorganize staff work groups or project teams
- sometimes accept the inevitable
- meet with the leaders and discuss negative effects
- if a serious problem, take to personnel committee of Board of Directors
- plan mixers, get people better acquainted

24. How do you get your staff to stop clumping on the playground and mix with the children?

- divide playground into areas, and assign a station to each staff member, with an extra staff person as a floater. If a staff person has to leave with a child, either the areas of responsibility change or the floater takes over.
- during staff meeting make a diagram:

```
ooo        x x        (Ask what is wrong
ooo         x         with this.)
o
```

- log accidents on playground and address accident patterns at a staff meeting
- have special activity plans for areas in playground
- change staff dynamics
- give staff time to meet with each other so they don't only meet on the playground
- have a large bell--as the director looks out the window and sees staff clumping, hit the bell
- emphasize active physical play in the program; staff observe and participate
- bring up at staff meeting the whole area of liability, and each person's responsibility to prevent it
- review playground rules with staff
- cultivate a trust between staff and director so that director acknowledges other legitimate concerns on playground, and doesn't assume all talk is idle chatter
- encourage staff to continue eye contact with children even when having a short conversation with another adult

25. How do you encourage staff to avoid waste of consumable materials, such as paper towels, paint, etc.?

- limit number of supplies assigned
- put classroom on "consumable supplies" budget
- offer bonus to staff for money not used from consumables
- plan fun event for staff from resources saved
- discuss alternatives at staff meeting
- brainstorm ways of conserving supplies
- encourage use of recyclable materials
- ask staff to prioritize use of materials (i.e.: construction paper for certain projects, but computer paper for drawing)
- lock up supplies
- have director in control of supplies and what they are used for
- write a humorous note--"The consumable fairy has disappeared."

26. How do you deal with individual staff who are absent often?

- set clear limitations
- give list of approved, recommended subs--have staff find own sub and report to director who it is
- have staff pay own sub
- use peer pressure
- use as topic for staff meeting--how to work with subs
- motivate
- job share
- inform that attendance may effect merit raise after 1/2 of sick leave days have been used
- recognize that new staff are especially susceptible to viral infections
- document when and why person is off and use for evaluation
- tolerate subs who will mess up their room
- post absences
- recommend flu shot

27. How do you handle tardiness--coming in late and coming back from lunch late?

- get a punch-in time clock
- document
- bring it up at a staff meeting and allow other staff to express their feelings; discuss how lateness effects the program as a whole
- have a sign-in-and-out log on director's desk
- dock salary for time not worked
- give warning, then terminate
- use promptness as a criteria during evaluations
- eliminate leaving the site for lunch (as a consequence)
- readjust time schedule
- remove person from that position
- discuss with person and find out reasons for tardiness

28. What do you do when staff do not get lesson plans done on time or complete other required tasks?

- provide paid planning time
- remind them of your expectations
- ask them "why"
- explain why it's necessary to have them done on time
- require them to hand them in on Thursday or Friday (for the following week), or 4-5 days ahead, etc.
- have staff present plans at staff meeting
- don't ignore, give feedback right after it happens
- cancel planned activity (like field trip) if not prepared for properly, and let staff deal with the consequences
- reprimand in written form
- check with staff during the week to see if lesson plans are being worked on
- verbally let the staff know you appreciate the work that goes into planning
- reward with a no-plan"fun week," when they don't have to do planning
- have a "left-over" week for using plans from past weeks that haven't been used (helps see plans as useful)
- use team-planning

29. How do you get staff to use prep time effectively?

- walk in on them (monitor)
- allow time during working hours, and explain the purpose--so they don't have to take work home
- help structure--give specific suggestions and provide with lots of resources
- have a weekly shared prep time to make classroom plans
- work in teams, in different areas
- use sign-up lists, so people can volunteer
- include as part of yearly evaluation
- compliment for results, in public and private
- relay parent compliments about activities
- team up experienced staff with new staff members

30. How do you keep a staff person when and where they are supposed to be?

- observe and document
- check in and out of classroom (use a special form)
- have another staff person monitor
- have clear cut written expectations
- stand by the teacher's door, be visibly obvious, and looking at watch
- discuss problems at staff meetings
- announce on P.A. system "you should all be in your classes"
- be accessible to staff
- let staff know you will be "making the rounds"
- point out importance of modeling; new staff look to experienced staff for guidance
- include in their evaluation

31. What do you do when a teacher has a classroom that is unsafe or unhealthy?

- point out immediately, as noticed
- cite regulations (city, state)
- have health consultant visit
- look for resources on safe classrooms (videos)
- provide hazard checklist
- do monthly classroom inspection, both staff and director, and then compare
- periodically set aside time at staff meetings to evaluate
- point out problem and consequences if there were to be an accident
- allow adequate time for classroom maintenance and improvements
- set specific standards for tidiness and safety
- team messy and tidy people together

32. What do you do when a teacher has a classroom that is not up-to-date ("fresh" materials, seasonal posters, etc.)

- send staff person out to observe another classroom
- pay for in-service training
- schedule classroom workday
- use peer pressure
- set up tours of classrooms in the building
- bring in outside visitors
- provide rotating awards for classroom of the week, with teachers deciding
- provide feedback from parents to staff
- set calendar for when room decoration expectations are due
- discuss expectations at staff orientation
- provide resource books on classroom ideas

33. How do you handle excessive phone usage by staff?

- put a time limit on phone calls
- limit number of calls
- take messages and have staff return calls on break except in emergency cases
- set a firm policy--"Our business depends on the availability of the telephone; please limit the number of calls."
- set a policy--"The center phone is a business phone and it is to be used for only the center business."
- install a pay phone
- have the phone on the director's desk
- charge for phone usage
- use a metered telephone service and have a log of phone usage
- allow for emergency or crisis situations

V. TEAMWORK ISSUES

34. How do you get your staff to work as a team?

- team-building workshop
- establish goal of what you want to accomplish, and keep everyone involved in the on-going process
- director, let go of control
- encourage joint planning
- pair up complimentary staff members
- when possible, allow staff to choose their co-workers
- have teacher participate in hiring of assistant teacher and aides for his/her classroom
- give teams time to get together and know each other
- encourage team projects

35. How do you mesh strengths/weaknesses of staff?

- draw out expertise at staff meetings--ask to do a specific task that they're strong in
- pair people together with opposite strengths
- look for strengths/weaknesses during interview; structure questions during interview to find strengths/weaknesses
- point out strengths to staff and ask them to do something in their area of strength
- assign responsibilities according to each staff person's strengths--so each has certain responsibilities matching strengths and areas of expertise
- try to take into consideration each personality when making staff placements
- be up front about each person's strengths/weaknesses during orientation
- focus on strengths; don't shame weaknesses
- focus on whole staff together (i.e.: "I'm good at this, so I'll do it." "I'm not good at this/I hate doing this, so someone else can do it."
- take staff away from school setting and see individual personalities emerge (less formal atmosphere)
- use a personality inventory with staff, discuss at staff meeting
- use low key activities to find out personal strengths and weaknesses within staff (use as a tool during staff meetings). For example, give staff a list of questions, each person getting answers from the others, thus finding out interests, as well as strengths and weaknesses of other staff

36. How do you get part-time teaching staff (assistants and aides) involved in the daily activities and long-term planning?

- have them read and initial daily log
- invite them to participate in staff meetings
- include in occasional staff meetings (for example, quarterly)
- record staff meetings (audio)
- assign full-time staff to report to half-time staff
- note activities of part-time staff in newsletter
- provide a form for part-time staff to write program ideas and suggestions and try to use the ideas
- use them as full-time subs
- have teachers assign specific activities for part-time staff to do
- require participation at full staff retreats
- involve in goal-setting planning meetings
- include as an item on their evaluation

VI. DIRECTOR/STAFF RELATIONSHIP

37. How does the staff know you are the director and not a peer?

- I write the checks--determine amount and sign
- I have a t-shirt that says "I am the buck-stopper"
- I have an office with a door on it
- I have an office upstairs
- I do the evaluations
- I "suggest" raises
- I tell them!
- I handle the "hard stuff"
- I solve the problems
- I lead the staff meetings
- I belong to a directors association
- I handle difficult visitors, the board, salespeople, crabby children, and crabby parents
- my professional attitude indicates this
- my professional appearance indicates this
- I supervise them
- I hired them and I can fire them

38. When are you friend and when are you boss? Do they blend?

- difficult to be real close friends
- can be friends with staff, but need a fine line
- communicate that "I need to do this as director."--can work with small staff
- with a large staff (like 30), must always be the boss
- you are friend when involves a personal problem of a staff person; you are boss if the problem involves the center; they blend if the personal problem affects the work setting
- tell staff at beginning that we work together, but the school does come first
- being a boss comes first; friendship may later develop or increase, but being a boss must come first
- state "putting friendship aside, we need to deal with this...."

39. What are some techniques to show empathy in supervising staff?

- use extensive verbal communication; explain pros and cons of issues
- explain why something is being done a certain way and state: "I understand, but as the director, I'm obligated to do...."
- try to guide the conversation and keep on professional level; ask questions "How is this affecting your job?" "What do you want me (director) to do?"
- ask questions of staff to clarify issues; try to be open about problems
- be a good listener; don't try to be a "fixer"
- observe staff and initiate conversation if something about a staff member concerns you
- check with staff and ask questions if you know they are having problems (i.e.: sick mother, going through divorce)

ORGANIZING

IN-SERVICE TRAINING
VACATION DAYS
FIELD TRIPS
SUPER DIRECTOR
PARENT HANDBOOK

ORGANIZATION

This section is concerned with the mechanics of setting up procedures to make functioning as a director easier. It focuses on the ways directors go about managing the routine parts of their job and includes all aspects of recruiting, hiring, and structuring of employment policies. Many hiring procedures have been subject to a great deal of change over time as data privacy laws and hiring practices change. Most directors have had to modify their practices to conform to current laws while still attempting to find qualified people to work with children. The answers reflect practices which conform to Minnesota state and federal law. Be sure to check on the laws in your state.

Preparation and planning are crucial in effective management and although directors' styles may vary, they all felt developing forms, checklists, detailed job descriptions, prepared questions, manuals, etc., helped them organize this quite overwhelming job. Although all of these things take time to develop initially, in the long run they save not only time, but energy and aggravation as well.

Also included in this section are those procedures designed to deal with managing the group aspects of the program such as structuring and handling staff meetings, dealing with the Board of Directors, time management, etc. Standard organizational procedures are important in making all of these run smoothly.

I. RECRUITMENT

1. What techniques are most successful for you in recruiting staff?

- send brochures to higher education, vo-tech schools
- advertise in newspapers (daily and neighborhood), church bulletins, employment services (state and private), temporary agencies
- ask other staff, ask parents, use word of mouth advertising
- ask other directors who recently hired new staff
- use nepotism (hire relatives--either your own or those of current staff)
- contact schools and teacher training centers
- share staff with another program
- use another center's part-time staff
- contact local professional organization (AEYC, Directors Association, resource groups, etc.)
- provide training for promising people on sub list
- entice trained teachers who want to be at home to work part-time and bring their children if appropriate

2. In a rural community, how do you recruit staff?

- another state
- church bulletins
- word of mouth
- local newspapers
- area vo-techs
- area high schools
- state job services at county level
- on-the-job-training programs
- friends
- parents
- past babysitters
- recommendations from others

3. **What's the first thing you do when you need to hire new staff?**

- cry!
- reevaluate hours
- redefine--look at existing staff for promotion
- evaluate job description
- keep active job file to draw from
- recruit from employment agency specializing in human resource field

4. Where can you advertise?

- college newspapers
- Christian radio stations
- community bulletin boards
- pediatricians' offices
- library
- personnel offices
- local newspaper
- college job placement service or bulletin board
- Directors Association newsletter

5. How do you find qualified substitutes (as opposed to just warm bodies)?

- don't let your staff get sick--pay for flu shots!
- maintain a school sub list, with names obtained from running newspaper ads, asking in church bulletins, interviewing, public school sub list
- use a professional substitute service
- ask director's group
- shift existing staff
- overstaff on a regular basis so it is still ok if one is absent
- current existing and support staff
- build up part-time staff so more people are available to fill in
- hire floaters and build the cost into the budget
- hire 1/2 time person to be used for anything
- find young people (16 or 17) and train them (start out in area like nap room, and gradually work into areas of more responsibility)
- keep an on-going active job file of acceptable job applicants
- students doing field experience
- students from local high school child development classes; college early education students; nanny school students
- parents; relatives; church members
- babysitters that parents employ
- community education teachers (ECFE program), school teachers

II. INTERVIEWS

6. How do you prepare for an interview?

- set aside time to prepare self and staff--go into seclusion for awhile
- acquaint self with applicant's file and job description
- reevaluate job description if necessary
- prepare packet for applicants, including: job description, mission statement, basic philosophy, benefit sheet
- prepare situational questions for each position; review questions while applicant is looking over packet
- ask same questions of all applicants; have desired answers in mind
- provide uninterrupted setting
- keep fair hiring practices in mind
- arrange time with children, if desired
- interview in a team; sometimes let staff help, either in initial interview or follow-up

7. What do you include on applications?**

- name, address, phone number
- place for teaching license number, social security number
- birthday (month and day only)
- past schooling/education
- specific early childhood classes taken
- professional organizations and memberships
- previous experience
- special interests and talents
- references, and may we contact?
- Employment Eligibility Verification (Form I-9)

**See Forms Kit for Directors for sample applications.

8.* What are some of your favorite interviewing questions?

a.) Personal questions:

- What would your current boss/former employer/family say about you?
- What would your peers at your last job say about you?
- Tell me about yourself.
- Are you willing to work with any age group you are not being interviewed for?
- Why do you think you would be happy in child care?
- What are some ways that you are flexible in your life?
- What activities are you involved in, in the community, the church, or in your family?
- Is there anything else you want to tell me about yourself?
- Are you willing to work for three hours on a trial basis, where you can see what it is like to work here, and we can see how you work with our children and staff?
- Are you going to stay longer than 6 months?
- What are your favorite activities with kids?
- What are your hobbies?
- Why did you choose this career or program?
- Do you play the piano?

*See Appendix

b.) **Program questions:**

- What do you do with a child who persists in biting others?
- What do you do if an ill child vomits at the lunch table?
- If a child has tipped over the easel, bitten a child, etc., how do you deal with this child? (Looking for answer to include checking to see if child is feeling well.)
- What do you feel makes a quality program for children?
- What are your feelings about touch and affection? What are you comfortable with?
- Two children are fighting over the same toy--how are you going to handle it?
- What do you do if a child comes to you and has painted himself purple?
- What do you see as your primary role as caregiver?
- What rules do you feel children need and how do you establish them?
- If you want children to play with playdough, how do you set up the activity? (Looking for answers about number of children, etc.)
- What would you do if you had to re-direct the behavior of a child?
- a hypothetical question regarding multicultural understanding and awareness

c.) **Communication questions:**

- What do you do when faced with a moody co-worker?
- Describe your supervisory style and how you would practice it.
- How do you deal with a staff member who uses techniques you disagree with?
- What do you feel your relationship role should be toward aide? assistant? teacher? parent? director?
- What would you do if an irate parent burst into the room?
- How would you tell a parent that their child consistently solves problems by hurting other children? (Or other hypothetical question dealing with parent communication.)
- What do you do when a co-worker writes a program rule and you disagree?
- How do you handle an overly assertive adult?
- How do you communicate with parents at pick-up time?
- How would you handle suspected abuse?
- If you've got 20 children ready to go to the zoo, with 4 parent volunteers ready to drive, and it starts to rain, what do you do?

9. **In the interview, how do you get them to tell you things that you can't legally ask?**

- consult an attorney
- What transportation plans would you make to get to the center on time? (Look for answer about dropping off children.)
- What provision do you have for your children if they get sick?
- We offer reduced tuition to children of the staff--would you be interested?
- We have a smoke-free environment. Is that a problem for you?
- In emergency situations, how long would it take you to get here?
- Do you have a degree? What year did you get it?
- Tell me about yourself. (Listen carefully and watch them divulge information that you can't ask.)
- Are you on any medication that would affect your work here?
- Have you ever had experience with child abuse?
- Tell me about your family.

10. How do you know when you receive an honest answer?

- gut reaction
- check references
- phrase question two different ways to see if answers are the same
- ask open-ended questions (ask "how...")
- look for eye contact; observe body language
- include a classroom observation; note questions asked
- keep in mind that good teachers may not interview well, so weigh heavily on in-classroom segment of process

11. What other things do you look for when qualifications of the staff are equal?

- future plans and how long she/he plans to stay
- commitment to the program; do they agree with the program's philosophy
- willingness to learn
- number of years experience and most recent experience
- review written responses to questions or items during interview
- consider ability to mold to center's philosophy; sometimes offsets amount of experience
- personality balancing with rest of staff
- flexibility in teamworking
- flexibility in hours
- reference responses
- answers to hypothetical questions on emergency situations
- how situational questions are answered
- extra things they do (i. e.: class B drivers' license, piano)
- outside interests unrelated to child care
- gut feeling
- don't hire relatives of staff if an alternative is available
- how do they respond to child-related material in the office (i. e.: posters, children's drawings, etc.)?

12. How do you use classroom observations in the interviewing process and what do you look for?

- call back for classroom experience after original interview; do same day if possible
- screen, then put in classroom for 2-3 hours to interact with children and team; ask for further questions from applicant; ask for input from staff
- observe body language of applicant
- let them observe for awhile, then participate as an active team member
- give them a specific area (i.e.: blocks, art) to supervise and let them go
- observe how they handle conflict among children
- have them lead a portion of circle time activity
- plan and implement a one-on-one activity
- interviewer sits in classroom to observe dynamics and reports to director
- hire as a sub first, if possible

13. How do you use staff input in the job interviewing process?

- have staff work with applicant
- ask for their reaction and be a good listener
- ask how did they work with the children?
- have staff sit in on interview (give them interview questions), and give them an evaluation to use on applicant
- have first interview with the director, and second interview with staff included
- or have one two-part interview, first with director; then with staff included
- have an understanding of what the current staff are looking for in an applicant (can be vague or get a specific list, including specific qualifications they would like in an applicant)
- have staff read through resumes and give reactions to director

14.* How do you handle reference checks for potential staff?

- structure questions you want to ask
- use some structured questions, some open-ended
- get written references
- do both written and phone references
- run police check or criminal check through sheriff's department (be sure you know if a fee is required)
- request permission to contact past employers
- get references both from direct supervisor and personnel department of previous employer
- talk informally with other directors if individual has worked in child care before

*See Appendix

III. STAFF SCHEDULES

15. Who covers the program when you are away?

- assistant director
- head teacher
- other staff
- lead teachers
- one person designated by director
- staff--responsibilities are divided; person with whom "the buck stops" is appointed; must be clear about duties, decision making process, and responsibilities
- board member
- rotate among staff
- select one responsible staff member, and train them to handle specified duties if/when you are unavailable

16. How do you schedule staff "shifts"?

- schedule using seniority for preferences
- set schedule--one person responsible for opening, one for closing
- add incentive pay, a little more for opening and closing shifts
- two staff people switch shifts, for example,

  MWF 9:30 - 6:30

  TTH 8:00 - 4:30
- share shifts--open two weeks, then close two weeks
- hire specifically for opening and closing
- schedule 4-day work weeks (10 hours/day), and rotate days off; staff members work out scheduling among themselves
- flexible schedules that change quarterly
- hire extra part-time help so can offer days/shifts off, or shorter days/shifts
- increase part-time employees, so more people to choose from when scheduling
- change scheduling at end of summer when public schools start

17. How do you handle breaks?

- 8 hours, 45 min. lunch and 45 min. prep time
- 8 hours, 1/2 hour break paid
- 8 hours, 1/2 hour break unpaid, can leave center
- more than 4 hours, 15 min. break
- floater (regular staff or hired specifically) to come in during morning breaks
- allow staff to schedule own breaks, within limits
- schedule prep time (not a break) during the 8 hour shift
- rotate job duties (nap room, "awake children", kitchen clean-up)
- director subs in classroom so staff can take breaks

18. How do you arrange vacations?

- one person at a time (first to ask, first granted) unless extenuating circumstances
- send out staff survey in the spring--time off (vacations), change shifts, variety of questions
- staff calendar to sign up on
- give option of summers off (ask non-working summer staff to sub during the summer)

IV. STAFF MEETINGS

19. Why are staff meetings important?

- to maintain communication
- to discuss problems
- to have a break away from children
- to give opinions
- to share information
- to maintain camaraderie
- to share insights about children and families
- to discuss behavior problems and determine consistent plans
- to review upcoming events
- to give praise for jobs well done

20. **How do you arrange staff meetings?**

- potluck dinner at someone's house, once a month, staff required to attend
- director provides dinner for evening staff meeting
- during nap time, weekly; someone hired to come in to free staff
- formal staff meetings every 6 weeks, team meetings every week
- staff meetings weekly and additional team meeting during the week
- special meetings--brainstorming meetings on 2-3 topics approximately 3 times a year
- vary meetings--some day, some evening
- staff are paid for staff meetings or get comp. time or informal leave time next day

21. Tips for a successful staff meeting

- start and end on time
- set agenda--offer time for changes then stick to it
- schedule on consistent days
- get staff input/consensus on time and location
- allow time for brainstorming--often most productive part of the meeting
- change leaders/facilitators
- solicit one idea from each person on topic of concern
- provide comfortable setting
- pay staff for staff meetings
- one staff member be recorder--rotate
- have food/treats
- no phone interruptions
- provide specified time for staff "show & tell"
- avoid long-run narratives--ask for written summary after point is made; defer to end of meeting to follow-up with details if time; provide opportunity at another time for embellishment
- invite input from all, so meeting not just a forum for director
- use a variety of approaches, sensing the needs of staff and director; be flexible
- post blank paper and invite suggestions for agenda, in addition to director's agenda

V. Communication (Director, Staff, Parents)

22. When can staff get together, to communicate about children, program, etc., or get to know each other?

- pay staff for coming in 1/2 hour early or at end of each day
- hire someone or have director come in during break/nap time, so that time can include meeting with co-workers
- have director cover during middle of day while staff meet together (proposed as a privilege, and when director can't do it, it doesn't happen)
- rotate planning of social events for staff
- start monthly staff meetings with social time
- once a month staff goes out to dinner on their own time; they pay; not a staff meeting; optional
- plan for one special "staff day" to clean rooms and closets

23. **How do you set up communication between staff and director regarding injured or sick children, broken equipment, etc.?**

- provide appropriate forms for notification
- establish procedure--staff reports to director who contacts parents
- point out consequences
- state procedures at orientation
- follow-up immediately on infraction
- provide daily log for all center activity, to report above instances, initialed by staff
- require written requests for equipment repair
- staff suffers consequences of broken equipment if not reported
- be responsive
- let staff know how you use information they give you

24. How do you communicate to staff the importance of turning in health forms?

- arrange for on-site examinations through hospital outreach
- tell them to bring in a form when they go to the doctor for any reason--hurt finger, pap test, whatever
- mark their staff file so it's noticed whenever reviewing the file
- mark the staff calendar with dates due
- at yearly evaluation time, review with them when they need it; emphasize it's their responsibility
- at staff meetings, give reminder 6 months before it's due
- make it a condition of employment

25. How, and by whom, are parent conferences conducted?

- team teachers--team of two do together
- team teachers--split group and each do half
- teacher and director together
- teacher and other consultant together
- first conference, emphasize social aspects, getting acquainted, developmental history
- pre-enrollment conference--home visit
- ask child "What things shall we tell your parent(s)?"
- use sample of child's work
- include children in conference
- exclude children from conference (provide space or child care if child comes unexpectedly)

26. How do you help staff conduct successful parent/teacher conferences?

- plan a staff meeting to discuss parent conferences to help relieve staff anxiety
- role play among staff
- develop teacher assessment materials
- instruct staff on how to evaluate
- observe other parent/teacher conferences
- watch a video of a well-done parent/teacher conference (training video)
- provide framework or structure for recording in the classroom and reporting (in notebook and then to parents)
- establish a procedure on how to gather materials for the childrens' files to show at conference
- provide books on parent communication
- state school expectations for individual conferences
- give parents some questions to answer about the child before the conference
- give parents an evaluation to complete after the conference
- plan parent/teacher conference before child is enrolled (pre-enrollment conference)

27. How do you prepare staff to deal with difficult parent encounters (such as irate parent, inebriated parent, unauthorized person)?

- have an in-service training for director and staff from outside professionals
- establish written policies and procedures
- print policies in parent handbook
- orient and train, especially staff who close at the end of the day
- role play possible situations
- instruct staff to invite person to come into office (away from children) if safe
- discuss proper authorities to call in specific situations
- try to have two people on staff at all times so you have help when necessary
- agree upon a hand signal that staff knows means "alert authorities!"
- copy car license number and notify authorities if the situation is unsafe for the child (such as a parent under the influence of chemicals, or an unauthorized person picks up)

VI. BENEFITS

28. What are some of the benefits you offer?

- the satisfaction of helping children grow and develop
- sick leave
- vacation time
- personal day plan--a combination of vacation, sick leave or other
- paid holidays
- mental health days
- religious holidays
- floating holidays
- funeral leave
- days off for severe weather (floods, blizzards, etc.)
- parenting leave
- compensatory time
- workers' compensation
- health insurance
- dental insurance
- life insurance
- disability insurance
- annuities
- profit-sharing plans; stock options
- investment plans
- participation in group buying plans
- continuing education paid for
- in-service training paid for
- free or reduced tuition for own children in program
- free meals and snacks
- company car (i.e.: van)

29. During lay-offs, how do you handle benefits?

- no benefits at all
- if program provides hospitalization, allow it to continue if you can afford it
- offer option of their paying own benefit expenses while laid off
- keep their anniversary date, so at least they don't lose seniority, and are eligible for vacation time, etc.

VII. TERMINATION/LAYOFF

30. What do you do when a staff member voluntarily leaves the program?

- tell them they can't leave until they find their own replacement
- rejoice or cry, depending on the situation
- get the resignation in written form*
- plan a party
  - invite former students
  - do a video about the school as a gift
  - have an open house
- schedule an exit interview
- if retiring, alert news media
- buy a gift (the center can purchase an AEYC poster or gift)
- give them an appreciation sculpture
- involve children---have them make a large sign; use children's artwork
- make up a photo book of "real photos"
- ask if they would be willing to sub or share expertise at future staff in-service

*See Appendix

31. What do you do when a staff member is fired?

- give monetary compensation and have them leave immediately
- have documented evidence
- send written notice to other staff; inform in a positive way
- immediately have a staff meeting
- inform parents in a positive way; reassure parents of center stability
- allow other staff to react
- know local and state laws of unemployment
- seek legal counsel regarding what you can and can't say (how to handle questions regarding reference questions)
- make sure you have temporary replacement available immediately
- give option to resign
- CYA (Cover Your Anatomy)

32. What questions do you ask in an exit interview when a staff member leaves?

- Will you share the reason why?
- Do you have suggestions or ideas for program improvement?
- What things did you enjoy the least?
- What changes would you like to see?
- What are your future plans?
- Will you be available to sub?

33. How do you handle cut-backs in staff caused by decreases in enrollment?

- have staff brainstorm solutions
- present options to staff
- cut back everyone's hours
- lay one person off (Draw straws? Ask for volunteers?)
- offer voluntary, temporary leave-of-absence
- try recruitment drive to increase enrollment
- have staff take vacation time
- use laid-off person as a sub
- recommend person to another program as a sub
- share person with another program during lay-off time (only share with a program you really trust!)

34. How do you handle references for former staff? What information can be released?

- consult state and federal regulations--they are forever changing
- if staff person has asked you to provide information, get permission from former employee in writing*
- can give positive response in writing
- there's a difference between on- and off-the-record; some things can't be said from your office but you can pass on the same information informally over lunch

*See Forms Kit for Directors for sample.

VIII. BOARD OF DIRECTORS

35. How do you work with your Board of Directors?

- with difficulty
- plan quiet time before board meeting to prepare
- define responsibilities of director and board
- have well defined by-laws
- planned agenda mailed in advance
- get necessary information to the board before the meeting so they can give director feedback and feel prepared
- introduce important items well in advance--introduce at one meeting and decide at the next
- involve non-parent community member
- educate the board
- keep the board informed and talk about issues and problems
- ask them to get personally involved so they begin to understand the situation
- listen to them, and then do things my way
- let the board know the distinction between day-to-day operations and over-all procedures
- provide in-service from outside
- plan to present things to the board--state clearly, without opinions; opinions may be offered after the issue has been presented
- document recommendations from other existing organizations
- help determine who will be on board--members with varied expertise. For example, one-third each of parents, church, and community representatives

- make board members realize their input is valuable
- include as board members those who will be helpful to you (i.e.: accountant, lawyer, health specialist, dietician, personnel manager, children's retail, marketing, etc.)

IX. PERSONAL MANAGEMENT STYLE

36. How does the director manage in a 40 hour week?

- use answering machine to limit/control phone time
- cordless phone
- beeper
- assistant director hired to cover extra hours
- hire extra staff to cover phones
- take comp. time for those 10-12 hour days
- take a long lunch hour when working a 10-12 hour day
- take a staff person to lunch once a week--that way you're forced to get out at noon
- force self out in middle of day if staying late
- take advantage of flexibility of director's schedule
- let go of "workaholic" feeling
- hire staff member as part-time assistant director
- learn to delegate
- recruit parent volunteers to help (i.e.: type newsletter, routine errands or tasks, etc.)

37. How do you get out from under all the piles of paper that are on your desk?

- hope for a strong wind to blow them away
- write down goals in order of importance
- make a list of things you will accomplish tomorrow
- make a new "tomorrow" list every day
- reach one goal before going on to next one
- delegate-delegate-delegate!
- break down big jobs into small workable parts
- return phone calls the same day, don't let them pile up
- act on or file all papers
- when you start to work on a file, finish
- hint: every time you take on someone else's problem, their problem is solved

38. How do you deal with constant interruptions?

- establish regular office hours
- establish clear procedures so staff can operate independently
- establish limits and be clear about interruptions you will not tolerate
- have an open/closed door policy
- hire a secretary or administrative assistant
- use an answering machine
- use a "do not disturb" sign
- work outside of the office
- establish rounds, you go to the staff rather than having them come to you
- set up short individual conferences
- tell long-winded staff to state their problem in two sentences
- encourage written statements of problems in a log book--saves time and you can prepare your response
- delegate all your responsibilities to someone else
- require that problems be brought to staff meetings

39. How do you avoid being a scapegoat?

- have a parent board
- have staff member follow-up on own suggestions
- refer to written policy; "It is the policy of the center...."
- give name of state licensor
- always try to give a reason; explain city or state regulations
- listen and let them verbalize reason
- explain "Insurance won't allow it."
- explain "Landlord/building owner won't allow it", "Church won't allow it", "It's against church policy", etc.
- explain it's not in the budget

40. How do you separate your personal and professional life?

- living a long distance from program--during half-hour drive coming and going I "gear up" and "change gears"
- having an unlisted phone number
- not giving out my home phone number
- informing staff that work is work and home is home
- working at home only during a designated time period
- not taking work home
- not living where I work; not working where I live
- having a separate set of friends not related to the field
- setting a tone--putting limits and boundaries on work (am I a workaholic?)
- take vacations
- post a sign on the door for uninterrupted time so I don't have to take work home

SUPPORTING

SUPPORT

Child care people tend to be nurturers and supporters by nature and indeed the hardest part for most directors is separating supervision from support. Often directors feel so supportive of staff that they wonder if their messages and supervisory expectations are clear and understood.

This section includes the interpersonal and educational aspects of the supervisory process. Often, this area feels the most comfortable; no doubt because it is the part of supervision most closely related to the teacher in us. Many successful directors have found ways of using and applying their teaching skills in this role. Almost without thinking, we start where the staff member is; helping them discover their talents, and encouraging the development of problem solving skills.

Staff growth and professional development is a large part of this role. In many ways the Director's job in encouraging staff development is made easier in Minnesota because a lot of on-going in-service training is required by the state's licensing law. You will therefore note many questions and answers relating to the facilitation of in-service training and ways to make it effective. Even if your state does not require in-service training, an agency or program can establish their own requirements. We would urge you to do so, keeping options and alternatives flexible. Remember, well-trained staff not only bring fresh ideas and enthusiasm to the program, but also gain a sense of professionalism and accomplishment.

I. STAFF MORALE

1. You know you can't please everyone, but how do you try?

- smile a lot
- encourage feedback from everybody
- effective listening
- accepting individual differences
- try to be open and flexible
- let staff follow-through on ideas even if you think they may not work out
- encourage staff to present new ideas for consideration
- change responsibilities within program so staff can try different areas
- discourage overtime
- encourage staff autonomy when appropriate
- give staff responsibilities for their classrooms and trust them to follow through (unless proven otherwise)

2. **What do you do to keep staff morale up?**

- keep staff informed
- include everyone on the staff as part of the team
- include staff in decision making process
- include staff representative on board of directors
- encourage and allow staff socializing during nap time
- have staff break room
- trust staff (once they have earned it) and show it
- staff outings outside of work (i.e.: bowling team, softball team)
- allow budgets for staff supplies
- give monthly spending allowances/petty cash
- center pays for staff in-service and other professional development (i.e.: college tuition) and allows for time off
- have staff plan their own "special treat" day

3. What do you do when you notice staff burn-out?

- plan a party
- buy them candy
- send them individual notes through the mail(!) and tell them how great I think they are
- give "perks"
- let choose next field trip
- give more responsibility
- TLC--praise them--"You're doing a great job."
- support
- talk
- listen
- give occasional "thank you"
- let them know they are appreciated
- give them time off to visit other programs
- allow them time away from children--to cook, do general organizing, etc.
- let staff switch positions
- feed them chocolate
- take staff out to lunch/dinner
- offer a mental health day, paid or unpaid
- let them know they can ask for time off

4. What are some inexpensive "perks" for staff?

a.) Within the center, no cost:

- write notes, be specific--"I noticed you did such-and-such
- recognize individuals and comment on what they do
- document the good, and use during evaluation
- staff appreciation days
- child care recognition days
- declare a "day" for a staff member
- teacher journals available for parents to write comments (i.e.: "thanks for your kindness when Katie hurt her knee")
- solicit good comments from parents
- give ownership of areas to teachers, so they can feel responsibility
- give them a supply budget each month
- involve staff in decisions that affect them (schedules, etc.)
- give option of not working for summer
- use volunteers to give breaks during nap time
- allow days off if staff person can find their own sub
- provide warm fuzzies at staff meetings
- have secret pals send something to each other each month
- visit classroom frequently
- give unscheduled break after hard situation

- pass on parent compliments, in front of rest of staff
- when attendance numbers are low, allow staff to rotate responsibilities to allow extra individual planning time

b.) Some cost to the center

- close for retreats (at a nice place, like a hotel with a pool)
- use subs for 1/2 day in a room at a time to give staff problem solving time, planning time
- close for 1-3 weeks for regrouping
- close for a mid-year mental health day
- make sick days available for mental health or other leave days
- give staff freedom to request time off
- allow days off without pay
- close for workshops and conferences
- staff select one staff member to send to conference
- close for an extra day (i.e.: the Friday before Labor Day weekend) so teachers can do classroom work without the children there
- encourage time off to do observations at other programs, and count time toward in-service training
- provide for in-service training time, with additional time for person to teach rest of staff what they learned
- pay for in-service training

c. Fun stuff, free or some cost to the center:

- give/send flowers/small gift
- raffle gift certificates, movie or sport tickets, etc.
- party for staff, arranged by parents (parents come in and supervise children, set up luncheon for staff)
- evening staff gatherings/dinner
- celebrate staff birthdays
- have pizza delivered
- have a "sunshine club"

5. **Besides money, how do you nurture your staff?**

- appreciate them and let them know how important they are
- if possible, give hours they want
- allow staff to sign up and select their own paid vacation days when possible
- sick days changed to personal days
- listen and support; be available; stand behind staff
- let staff know you stand behind them
- use teams together that nurture one another
- have a board for listing only positive comments between staff members
- budget some money for staff development
- have an on-going fundraiser for the staff to help them pay for the expenses at state or national AEYC conferences
- retreat for staff during winter
- have staff room equipped with such things as t.v., microwave, vending machine, coffee maker, hot tub
- provide a place for privacy when using the telephone
- oral and written compliments--on-going, not just at evaluation time
- little notes
- articles in newsletter about individual staff members
- inform board of special staff accomplishments so they can praise

- inform parents/acknowledge to parents that teachers are doing a good job (be specific)
- provide good benefits, like reduced tuition for their child(ren) enrolled in your program
- offer full benefits if person works more than 5 hours/day

6. How do you celebrate birthdays and other special occasions?

- the director never gets involved--center is too large
- director brings in treats
- treats are provided on a rotating basis--most recent birthday persons brings treats for the next
- birthday person brings in treats for staff and children
- birthdays acknowledged at staff meetings
- staff takes up a collection and buys presents for each other
- cards are circulated to be signed by all staff
- children make a big card
- book or record is bought for the school, in honor of the birthday
- one staff member, who enjoys doing it, is assigned to keep track, buy cards and treats for all birthdays (except his/her own)

7. Do you have a special event that the staff does annually?

- retreat in winter/fall
- Christmas party
- annual clean-up and lunch
- paid dinner
- lunch out in spring
- team-building in-service
- state conference socialization
- staff recognition during Week of the Young Child
- orientation luncheon
- "kick-off" in fall
- evaluation luncheon at end of nursery school year

8.* How do you motivate non-teaching staff (cooks, janitors, secretaries)?

- have a support staff appreciation day
- include an article about them in the newsletter
- let them know their work is appreciated
- invite them into the classrooms to introduce themselves and share what they do
- consider them for a bonus
- put their picture up on the bulletin board*
- include them on a staff biography page in the parent handbook
- recognize their good work in written form (short notes, etc.)

*See Appendix

9. How do you increase school spirit?

- have an annual pot-luck dinner or picnic
- have an annual parent-children-staff breakfast
- have once a month family nights
- offer parenting classes at the center
- set up a mentor program, pairing experienced and new staff
- serve coffee and rolls for parents during special times (i.e.: Christmas, Week of the Young Child)
- have special events (i.e.: Winter Carnival, Halloween Party)
- get lots of publicity in community newspapers
- have t-shirts or tote bags printed with the school logo, and sell or provide to families
- display on-going photos of center activities
- participate in charitable fundraisers

II. STAFF GROWTH/PROFESSIONAL DEVELOPMENT

10. How does your staff continue to keep up-to-date with early childhood issues?

- attending in-service training
- attending state Association for the Education of Young Children Conference
- reading articles I give them with their monthly paychecks (i.e.: articles from Young Children or Pre-K Today, etc.)
- reading periodicals (director sometimes highlights articles)
- reading association newsletters, routinely routed to them
- sharing in-service information with rest of the staff
- belonging to professional organizations
- discussing issues I bring up at staff meetings
- having time allotted at staff meetings for in-service training
- visiting other programs

11. How do you encourage professional growth for staff?

- pay for in-service and subs
- keep folder of training opportunities
- provide time to share what others have learned from classes and workshops
- have professional growth be a part of evaluation--take into account when someone has taken more classes than required
- compensate with salary adjustment when person goes beyond in-service requirements; make it a staff policy
- recognize person as a source of ideas; follow through with what they bring back; ask person to do an in-service training for rest of staff
- director supplies staff with both personal and professional growth opportunities and information
- bring consultants to do staff training on-site for whole staff

12. How do you get staff to keep up with in-service training?

- hound them!; give weekly reminders
- make it clear that it's part of the job requirement (state licensing rule or accreditation status)
- post all information on classes/conferences available
- individually tell staff about a class they might particularly be interested in
- give set number of educational leave days per year
- give equal number of hours off for number of in-service hours
- include in-service in contract to renew job position
- prepare and have signed a contract with specific dates and dollar amounts, done annually
- include in contract that staff must reimburse the center if they don't attend the class
- cut staff hours if don't meet requirements
- pay for required in-services
- give other incentives for training over minimum requirement
- provide for on-site training to make it easier
- provide child care for staff to attend in-service

13. **How do you reimburse for in-service?**

- reimburse for class upon completion of class
- reimburse only for required number of hours
- reimburse for in-service once a year, on their anniversary date of being hired
- keep a running total of hours and classes and reimburse annually--good time is right before licensing
- reimburse various amounts (i.e.: half cost of class during work hours, full cost if class taken on personal time, etc.)

14. What are good ideas for in-service training?

- bring in specialists at staff meetings or other times
- parents (to speak on area of expertise, or inform staff of their culture, etc.)
- public health nurses
- librarians
- church members
- observe at other sites
- classes at local vo-tech, colleges, universities, community education programs, medical clinics
- conferences
- VCR movies/cassettes
- educational television
- filmstrips
- read a book and give a report
- support group programs

15. How do you let parents/observers know about your staff's background and credentials?

- school newsletter
- bulletin board with pictures and descriptions*
- "introducing our staff" page or packet in parent handbook
- pair up staff and have them write about each other for the newsletter
- introductory video
- individual classroom pictures with descriptions of staff that are assigned to that room
- potluck suppers etc. with staff introductions given
- special welcoming day for new staff.

*See Appendix

III. SUPPORT FOR DIRECTORS

16. How does the director get support?

- director can shut door
- utilize parent evaluation form
- ask for it; tell staff "I need some support"
- join association
- join directors' support group
- set aside time to meet with other directors regularly
- keep communication with staff open
- solicit support from board
- keep refreshing own self--workshops and seminars
- have freedom to say "Don't bother me today".

17. In a small community, how can directors support each other?

- be in contact with each other--state-wide AEYC listings could help
- joining state organizations
- driving "all that way" into the metro area for association/support meetings
- carpooling to metro area
- monthly local meetings--breakfasts, lunches, mid-night snacks
- make an effort to meet new people
- calling other directors
  - to visit (network)
  - to inform of "interesting" items
  - to discuss problems

18. What do you do when you feel burnt out in your job?

- try to have fun in my personal life
- go walking
- when I close my door I make myself turn my head off
- swim
- do strenuous exercise/do aerobic dancing
- go on a retreat--any kind
- think of last May, when last session ended
- work in a nine-month program
- talk to somebody (discuss with good active listener who can relate)
- call a friend in the field
- call another director I met at the directors' support group
- call my mother
- go to the bakery
- leave--go out for lunch, etc.
- spend money--buy something for the center or my office
- ask for uninterrupted time to talk
- make internal changes
- get a co-director
- lighten up time requirements
- take one day at a time
- delegate responsibility
- make sure expectations are reasonable; lower my expectations
- reassess how long I will continue in my job; is it time to move on?
- realize I'm not indispensable

APPENDIX

Reference to Section 1, Question 1

EMPLOYEE PACKET

To Include:

1. Personnel Policies
2. Personnel Information Sheet
3. Medical Form
4. Job Description - copy given and reviewed
5. Statement about Center's Philosophy
6. School Policy Information
7. Accident Policy
8. Daily Health Inspection Procedure
9. Policy for Illness
10. Fire Drill Procedures
11. First Aid Procedures
12. Copy of Injury Report Form
13. W-4 Form filled out
14. Form I-9 filled out

Reference Section 1, Question 1

NEW STAFF ORIENTATION CHECKLIST

Employee Name ____________

Position____________________

Starting date_______________

Orientation date(s)__________

____ 1. During a walking tour of the center, go over the following:
   a. location of supplies and information (first aid supplies, staff and parent bulletin boards, appropriate files, staff bathroom and coatroom)
   b. classroom safety guidelines and rules
   c. big room safety guidelines and rules
   d. outdoor safety guidelines and rules

____ 2. Introduce to staff and explain responsibilities, grouping of children, and ratios

____ 3. Review schedule.

____ 4. Review discipline procedures and the employee's role in discipline.

____ 5. Mention any current special health or other concerns for individual children.

____ 6. Interactions with parents and employee's role.

____ 7. Cases of suspected child abuse, report to director privately.

____ 8. Ilnesses and first aid procedures.

____ 9. Mealtime guidelines.

____ 10. Bathrooming guidelines and changing children's clothes.

____ 11. Naptime guidelines

____ 12. Staff meetings, in-service classes, and a desire to learn.

____ 13. Staff evaluations and support by and for staff members.

____ 14. Location of fuse box, fire alarm, and fire extinquisher.

____ 15. Asking questions--no question is a dumb question.

Reference for Section 1, Question 4

SUGGESTED EVALUATION CRITERIA FOR PART-TIME STAFF

Reliable

- Is punctual
- Shows responsible attitude toward scheduled hours
- Plans ahead to allow time off for study and other activities

Children

- Relates to and respects children as individuals
- Works to develop child's positive self-concept
- Contributes to child's language development by talking with them
- Displays warmth and affection toward the children
- Shows enthusiasm and enjoyment of children
- Shows consistency in responding to children

Teaching Skills

- Is active and observant
- Able to discriminate between appropriate and inappropriate behavior
- Deals with problem situations effectively
- Initiates spontaneous group activities (Bingo, Simon Says)
- Works well with groups of children
- Encourages imaginative and constructive use of materials and equipment

- Prevents destructive use of materials and equipment
- Shares responsibility for room maintenance
- Is appropriately clear and firm when required
- Plans and leads "group time" activities
- Relays information to staff and head teacher, written or verbal

Attitudes

- Shows a desire to improve teaching skills
- Shows enthusiasm toward job
- Communicates with other staff and head teacher
- Works cooperatively as a member of a "team"
- Conveys a positive attitude about the children and the center
- Asks questions and otherwise shows a desire to learn about the children and the center

Adapted from First Trinity Creative Child Care, St. Paul, MN

Reference for Section 1, Question 4

SUGGESTED EVALUATION CRITERIA FOR AFTER SCHOOL STAFF

Program Responsibilities

- Is aware of total classroom
- Helps keep environment clean, neat and safe
- Supervises playground adequately
- Demonstrates flexibility

Relationship with Children

- Aware of and sensitive to individual needs of children
- Assists children in engaging in appropriate and meaningful activities
- Treats all equally and fairly
- Provides a good model
- Available at child's level
- Handles group time appropriately
- Fosters cooperation
- Anticipates potential problems
- Is patient and calm with children

Relationship with Parents

- Maintains a positive and pleasant attitude with parents
- Communicates effectively with parents

Personal/Professional Behavior

- Relates positively with staff
- Does not socialize with other staff when responsible for children
- Appropriate voice level
- Cooperative
- Assertive when necessary
- Responds promptly and appropriately to situations requiring supervision
- Seeks to expand knowledge of child development issues
- Carries through with suggestions from supervisors
- Is reliable
- Wears appropriate attire
- Follows procedures for requesting time off
- Keeps informed of school activities
- Appropriately handles situations with sick or injured children
- Keeps personal phone calls to a minimum
- Is enthusiastic

Reference for Section 1, Question 4

SUGGESTED EVALUATION CRITERIA FOR HEAD TEACHER

1. Teacher maintains a tactful and supportive relationship with each child.

2. Teacher considers children's individual needs and the needs of the group in his/her planning.

3. Teacher provides activities which are age appropriate for the whole group.

4. Teacher plans and carries out a balanced curriculum for his/her group.

5. Teacher introduces new experiences through special projects, field trips and guests.

6. Teacher observes and records individual children's progress for the children in his/her group.

7. Teacher prepares for and carries out parent conference twice yearly and as needed or requested.

8. Teacher communicates with parents on an on-going basis.

9. Teacher explains and enforces limits on children's behavior clearly and effectively.

10. Teacher makes suggestions and otherwise helps improve the center's program as a whole.

11. Teacher maintains a safe, attractive and neat classroom environment.

12. Teacher helps maintain a safe and clean environment in the center as a whole.

13. Teacher complies with center's health and safety procedures and helps in all emergencies.

14. Teacher helps supervise part-time staff appropriately.

15. Teacher maintains an honest supportive relationship with the director.

16. Teacher works well as part of a team.

17. Teacher uses discretion and consideration in conversations with and about staff, parents, and children.

18. Teacher goes on and off duty at the scheduled times.

19. Teacher makes conscientious use of vacation time and sick leave.

20. Teacher makes conscientious use of preparation time.

Adapted from First Trinity Creative Child Care, St. Paul, MN

Reference for Section 1, Question 5

SALARY EVALUATION

NAME OF EMPLOYEE________________________
POSITION__________________________________

Rate employee on the following criteria:

I. Knowledge of responsibility
II. Interaction with parents/children
III. Human relations
IV. Environment
V. Management skills
VI. Planning

Current Salary + Merit + Promotion = New Salary

____________ _____ _________ __________

______________________ __________
Signature of Evaluator Date

______________________ __________
Signature of Employee Date

Adapted from **Forms Kit for Directors**

Reference for Section 1, Question 8

DIRECTOR EVALUATION BY STAFF

Since we are all interested in expanding skills, we would appreciate your feedback in evaluating the director's role in the operation of your school. Please respond to this form based on your perception of how your director handles the following areas:

Rating Scale: 1...2...3...4...5...6...7...8...9...10
Need for improvement Excellent

1. Public relations and miscellaneous:
   a. Working with visitors, observers, students, volunteers
   b. Oversees all school functions: Orientation, Open House, Parent Night, Conferences, Workshops
   c. Health and safety procedures and policies implemented: Fire drills, emergency log, first aid box, medication forms, etc.
   d. Assists staff in completing personnel files: updating classes, first aid, personal papers.

2. Liaison for staff:
   a. Available to staff
   b. Supportive of staff needs and interests
   c. Provides a positive link between staff members
   d. Conveys important information in a timely and constructive way
   e. Acts as a liaison between staff and parents, relays parents concerns, suggestions, etc.

f. Encourages staff in their professional development
g. Develops and implements successful routines involving prep times, breaks, etc.
h. Divides staff responsibilities equally

3. Program needs:
   a. Is sensitive to needs of all programs within school
   b. Provides needed materials, equipment and supplies
   c. Oversees classrooms and provides leadership in their functioning

Reference for Section 1, Question 13

WARNING NOTICE

Name ____________________________ Date ____________

Job Description__________________ Branch__________

The _____________________ Center is desirous of giving all employees every reasonable opportunity to correct unsatisfactory work performance, or unsatisfactory conduct of a correctable nature if the employee evidences an earnest desire to improve. This warning notice now becomes a matter of records, and you will have an opportunity to correct the condition described below.

Any repetition or continuation of conduct or action on your part which is contrary to established rules and regulations, or which is detrimental to the best interests of the _____________________ or its employees will result in suspension from employment without pay, or termination of employment.

Reason for this Warning Notice___________________________

____

____

____

I have read and understand the above.

_________________________   _________________________

Employee's Signature   Director's Signature

Prepare in triplicate. Insert the original in the employee's folder. The first carbon should be given to the Personnel Office, and the second should be given to the employee.

Reference for Section 2, Question 8

More possible questions to use for interviewing:

1. Do you like children?
2. What do you like most about children?
3. What do you like least about children?
4. Describe what, for you, would be an ideal job.
5. What part of your last/present position did you like best/least?
6. How would you describe your relationship with your last supervisor?
7. What are the rewards/benefits of working in early childhood education?
8. Are you an enthusiastic person?
9. Does your enthusiasm show?
10. Have you done lesson planning?
11. Have you ever conducted parent conferences?
12. Are you able to remain calm when presented with the following:

    choking — diarrhea
    vomiting — accidents
    blood — severe storms

13. What are your teaching strengths/weaknesses?

Reference for Section 2, Question 14

REFERENCE REQUEST

TO: ________________________ Date: ________

____________________________ is being considered to fill a staff vacancy. Your name has been given to use as a reference. We would appreciate your personal and professional evaluation of the applicant. The information will be treated with the utmost confidence. Your cooperation is deeply appreciated.

____
Director

* * * * * * * * * * *

Please comment on the following:

PROFESSIONAL CRITERIA (Instructional Techniques, Conduct, Classroom Management, Parental Contacts, Understanding of Children, etc.)

PERSONAL CRITERIA (Creativity, Dependability, Writing Ability, Leadership, Judgement, etc.)

____________________ ____________
Signature Date
Address:

Adapted from **Forms Kit for Directors**

Reference for Section 2, Question 30

RESIGNATION OF EMPLOYMENT FORM

Please accept notice of my resignation from employment.

This resignation effective: ______________________

The reason for my decision is:____________________

____

____

____

____

Director______________

Employee____________

Date_________________

Reference for Section 3, Question 8

Staff Members,

We are in the process of making a display board with a picture and brief introduction of all our school staff. This is most helpful in assisting parents in identifying everyone who works here. Please fill in the brief description below and return it to your coordinator.

NAME:______________________________________

POSITION:__________________________________

WORK EXPERIENCE RELATED TO
CHILDREN:__________________________________

BEGAN WORKING AT OUR SCHOOL
(year):_______________________

Reference for Section 3, Question 15

Dear Staff:

In order to assist our families in recognizing their children's teachers, we will be displaying a pictorial bulletin board of our classroom teachers. Please fill out this form and return by mid-August at the latest. Be sure and enclose a photo of yourself (4 x 6 or slightly larger)

If you teach in two environments, we will need two photos

NAME:

CLASSROOM:

EDUCATIONAL BACKGROUND:

WORK EXPERIENCE (related field)

BEGAN TEACHING AT OUR SCHOOL:

RESOURCES

FOR

DIRECTORS

SOME RESOURCES FOR DIRECTORS

An Ounce of Prevention: An Administrative Guide for Directors - Norma Giaz, Ed.D., and Don Hall, Ed.D., published by Training in Abuse-Prevention (TAP) in West Virginia

Includes practical advice on selecting and supervising staff, team management and dealing with child abuse. Contact Region III Child Development Services, 10th Avenue and Bruce Street, Huntington, WV 25701.

Nursery School Day Care Center Management Guide - Clare Cherry, David S. Lake Publishers, second revised edition, 1986.

The One-Minute Manager - Kenneth Blanchard, William Morrow Publishing, 1982.

Survival Skills for Managers - Marlene Wilson, Volunteer Management Associates, 1981.

Leaders: The Strategies for Taking Charge - Warren Bennis and Burt Nanuc, Harper and Row, New York, 1985.

Day Care Personnel Management - Nancy Travis and Joe Perrault, Save the Children, 1981.

The Motivating Leader - Lewis Losoncy, Prentice-Hall, 1985.

Managing and Organization - Caplow Theodore, Holt, Reinhart and Winston, New York, 1983.

Supervision in Early Childhood Education, - Joseph Caruso, Teachers College Press, 1986.

Leadership and Learning: Personal Change in a Professional Setting - Barry C Jentz and Joan Woffard,McGraw-Hill, New York, 1979.

Planning and Administering Early Childhood Programs, 3rd edition - Celia Decker and John R. Decker, Charles E. Merrill Publishing, 1984.

JOURNALS

Child Care Information Exchange (P. O. Box 2980 Redmond, Washington, 98052; 6 issues/year)

Day Care and Early Education (Human Sciences Press, 72 Fifth Avenue, New York, NY 10011; 4 issues/year)

AFTERWORD

We hope our suggestions have given you new ideas and approaches to the problems you face on a daily basis. Support is greatly needed for all nursery school and child care center directors, and we encourage you to add to our lists of possible solutions.

Other books that have been published by E.C.D.A. are:

- Survival Kit for Directors, 1983. This is a collection of problem solving ideas gathered from sixteen Early Childhood Directors.

- Forms Kit for Directors, 1986. This is a compilation of 150 reproducible forms that include the following topics: Administration, Consent, Curriculum, Evaluation, Health/Safety/Medical, Infant/Toddler, Observations, Intake and Registration, and Staff.

Watch for future publications from the Early Childhood Directors Association.